WHAT KIND
OF A
HOUSE IS THAT?

By Harry Devlin

Parents' Magazine Press • New York

To my son, Brion Phillip Devlin

I also want to express my thanks to all the
kind and enthusiastic people who have made the
book a possibility and especially to Dr. Kenneth MacKay.

CONTENTS

AN ELEPHANT HOUSE

Eggs and Long Island ducklings for sale here

Flagship has been restaurant, store, and night club. It only gets wet when it rains.

Lucy's red-rimmed eyes have been staring out over the Atlantic since 1885 when the last sheets of metal were fastened to her back. Then she was a sensational attraction that "brought intelligent and traveled visitors from this and foreign countries." At one time, Lucy was "fitted out with studied effort to gratify a curious public" and was filled with "fitting mementos worthy of any bazaar." For a time she was a real estate office, a hotel and, only a short time ago, she was a home. Perhaps the family who lived in Lucy grew tired of living out of a trunk because today she broods alone and the doors in her rear legs are boarded shut. Lucy's bright colors have faded and her hide could use a good tinsmith. In fact, her future is very uncertain.

In Lucy's hey-day, two million people tramped the circular staircases in the hind legs through a series of 350 steps to the four bedrooms, reception room, dining room and howdah. Visitors looked out over the Atlantic through 22 windows and could see, from the howdah on Lucy's back, all the way from Margate to Atlantic City and Cape May.

Once Lucy had two identical sisters in Coney Island, New York, and in Cape May, New Jersey. The Cape May elephant was washed out to sea and the Coney Island sister caught fire.

The elephants were all the brain-children of James V. Lafferty who had in mind a colossal real estate office from which he could sell vacation lots to summer visitors. History doesn't tell us how he made out, but we do have some statistics on what it takes to make an elephant:

A million pieces of timber, 8,560 ribs or arches, 200 kegs of nails, 4 tons of bolts and bars and 12,000 square feet of sheet metal to cover it.

We also know that:

Lucy is 80 feet around the waist, 38 feet from head to tail; her legs are a trim 10 feet in diameter; her ears are 17 feet long and weigh 2,000 pounds each; her eyes are 18 inches in diameter and, finally, her tusks are 22 feet long.

Mr. Lafferty was undoubtedly inspired by the success of Jumbo, P. T. Barnum's giant pachyderm. Jumbo earned the great showman huge sums as an attraction and became a symbol for anything gargantuan.

America has always had some understanding of the eccentric. Our highways are lined with ungainly three-story ice cream cones, enormous hot dogs and other pop-art monuments. One of the most famous restaurants in Hollywood is a house-sized brown derby hat. Pictured here is a Long Island duck from which ducks are sold, and a flagship that only gets wet when it rains. The architecture? American Eccentric.

A MODEL HOME

The history of art, music and literature tells us that classical eras are followed by romantic eras which are then superseded by classical eras and other romantic eras. Classicism is characterized by clarity, simplicity, objectivity, restraint and balance. Romanticism loves the remote and the indefinite. Grandeur, passion and picturesqueness are its hallmarks. The romantic's dreams are boundless. Most of the eighteenth century art, music and literature was classical, but towards the end of that century a romantic wave swept Europe. Gothic poetry, literature and neo-Gothic architecture became a passion to people with the time and perception to be aware. In England, wealthy men built Gothic ruins of painted canvas very much like stage sets. Some even built permanent ruins in stone.

The height of romantic excess was reached in 1796 when William Beckford built an entire "ruined" abbey. Its octagonal tower was 276 feet high, its hall 120 feet high, and with its two wings it stretched 400 feet long. To build it, five or six hundred workmen worked through the nights by the light of huge bonfires. One night in 1825, the tower, built on faulty foundations, sank into the earth. Today, hardly a trace of Fonthill Abbey remains. That was real romanticism!

Much of America's romantic era coincided with the Victorian age. Edgar Allan Poe and Nathaniel Hawthorne led the way in literature and the Hudson River school of painters furthered it in art. Our architects made splendid contributions to a romantic setting with the Gothic, the Italianate and other revival forms.

The beautiful American Gothic house shown here was very much a part of the American romantic era. It was built as a model home in 1857 by Llewellyn Haskell to attract people to his new community of "cascades, flower gardens, winding roads and rambles." The project was very ambitious and very successful. In later days, Thomas Edison and many other distinguished Americans made their homes near our house and the community still flourishes.

Mr. Haskell made wise decisions. He hired one of the nation's best romantic architects, Alexander Jackson Davis, to design the model home.

The cottage, for so houses of this nature were called, was first lived in by Edward W. Nicholls, an outstanding Hudson River school painter. Later, it was the boyhood home of the great architect, Charles Follen McKim, the founder of the famous architectural firm, McKim, Mead and White.

Many books on architecture choose the Nicholls cottage as a splendid example of the domestic Gothic style. It lacks only bargeboards at the eaves to be a perfect example. It is now beautifully preserved by a family who understands its value as a cultural monument.

Rotch "cottage" in New Bedford, Massachusetts, is also by Alexander Jackson Davis.

A FUN HOUSE

*That's not a stork.
It's an ibis up there.*

*Washington Irving's Sunny-
side has stepped gables, too.*

In Cambridge, Massachusetts, in a triangle just outside the Harvard University Yard, stands one of the most whimsical buildings in the nation. It has a face and wears a hat with an enormous finial topped by an incredible ibis. And a lot of funny business goes on inside.

The fun house is the home of the *Harvard Lampoon*, both a club and a collegiate humor magazine. Members of the *Lampoon* are called "Poonsters" and they can enjoy the Thursday Dinners and other wildly social events at the clubhouse only if they perform in some capacity to publish the monthly magazine. If ties are worn at all, black club ties with horizontal purple and gold stripes identify a Poonster. Members are best identified by a certain irreverent air.

The building was begun in 1909, following a number of very prosperous years of publishing in which every issue was sold to students and others who stood in line to get the latest, most scandalous issue of all.

Before the present headquarters was built, the *Lampoon* held forth in a series of unbelievable lofts, dives, parlors and joints.

The *Lampoon* is not the oldest of the college magazines, but it has published continuously since 1876 and in the beginning aspired to be another *Punch*. *Punch* is the venerable British humor and literary magazine still very much alive and probing.

Some of the humor that thrives at the *Lampoon* goes astray and finds victims in unexpected places. One president of the *Lampoon*, dressed in a blond wig and other symbols of the coed, entered the annual Wellesley Hoop Race, won it, was found out and thrown into a convenient lake by the outraged Wellesley girls. A Poonster, masquerading as Adelbert Ames III, broke into the gruelling Boston Marathon race three blocks from the finish and was awarded a medal for Fourth Place.

College humor magazines have produced some of the great names in the literary and dramatic fields. The *Lampoon* has been one of the richest contributors, giving us an inheritance of authors, playwrights, philosophers and editors. Owen Wister, Robert Benchley, William Randolph Hearst and Robert Sherwood are only a few. Even the author of *Casey at the Bat*, Ernest Lawrence Thayer, was a Poonster.

The building itself draws on a number of architectural styles. The architect who built it considered it to be sixteenth-century Dutch. The stepped gables are certainly Dutch, but the large windows are English Collegiate Gothic. The dome of the building was originally ribbed with heavy Dutch tiles, but they have been replaced with copper which turns green when exposed to the weather.

Although the building is a twentieth century construction, it is eclectic — a combination of many archaic forms. Eclecticism is a nineteenth century hallmark and because it expresses a yearning for the past, it is a romantic era symbol.

A MILL

The history of day-to-day life in America is linked closely to the mill. It was at the heart of industry and agriculture from the beginning. In colonial days, the production of the mills meant reprieve from the backbreaking, time-consuming tasks of grinding grain by mortar and pestle. In later years, the mills made possible the mass production of cloth and grain and other items that permitted the expansion of the nation.

The mill itself is a marvel of eighteenth and nineteenth century initiative and ingenuity. All the power is derived from the pressure of water against the blades of the mill wheel. This power is transferred by gears, pulleys, belts and screws to perform a multitude of tasks ranging from the grinding of grain to the manufacture of nails.

Not all mills were water powered.

To the American colonists, the fiber plant called flax was essential to existence and the plant serves well to point up the importance of the mill. To make the summer clothing of one family, it took an acre of virgin soil to grow a sufficient quantity of flax. The flax was rotted, shredded and eventually spun and woven into linen cloth. The seeds and other leftovers were taken to the mill to be pressed by heavy stone wheels turning on a stone drum. Linseed oil resulted and it was useful to the colonist for cooking purposes, to light his lamps and to protect his tools from rust. Boiled linseed oil was used in his paint and as an important ingredient in his varnishes. What was left over, the miller compressed into feed cakes for cattle.

But the mill's functions went far beyond the pressing of oils. Heavy millstones ground endless tons of grain for flour and grist. Flour mills ground grain for human food and grist mills ground grain for animal consumption. Gypsum was ground to make the plaster which was spread to revitalize overworked soil. The woad or indigo plant was milled to a fine paste to make blue dye for clothing.

In the seventeenth and eighteenth centuries, nails, which had to be laboriously formed by the blacksmith's hammer, were so costly that a farmer moving west would often burn down his buildings to retrieve his nails. To discourage this, the governor of Virginia gave migrating planters as many nails as his house contained to save the building for other settlers.

Mini mill still works in Guildhall, Vermont.

The mill changed that. Sheets of iron 1/8″ thick by 2¾″ wide were fed into a mill-operated cutter similar to the giant paper cutters that bookbinders use to trim books. The nails were sheared off at the end of the sheet, and by 1825 were being produced in such quantity that nails were at last expendable.

Our red mill is in Clinton, New Jersey, and is now an historical museum. Happily, all the wonderful wooden machinery is intact and may be inspected by the public. Its record is remarkable in that it has served mankind since 1763, processing flaxseed oil, graphite, lime, talc and flour. In the twentieth century its wood and steel wheel·generated power for Clinton's first electric lights.

A ROUND SCHOOLHOUSE

Brookline, Vermont, is a remote place in a lovely valley. In the years before the Civil War it was a busy agricultural community, but generations of young people have drifted away and now only a few families remain. There is only one public building left. The little round schoolhouse is no longer used as a school, but it served well and honorably for more than one hundred years.

The round schoolhouse was built in 1821 of brick and heavy, hand-hewn rafters rising to a central peak. Because the heavy roof construction exerted dangerous outward pressure on the circular walls, a great, iron rod, an inch in thickness, girds the building just below the eaves. Since the building is 40 feet in diameter, the rod is more than 120 feet long.

Captain Thunderbolt alias Dr. John Wilson

The building was originally heated by a sheet-iron stove placed in the center of the single room which accommodated a master's desk, a circle of oak benches around the inside perimeter of the room, sixty smaller desks and a handful of hickory "discouragers." For eighty-seven years there were no repairs to this rugged little building. In 1910, the shed to the right was added to it.

The schoolhouse was built by the town fathers at the suggestion of Doctor John Wilson who had appeared as though from nowhere in 1821. He was a tall, commanding man who indicated that he had come from Boston. Since he was obviously a man of education, he was eagerly accepted by the residents of the West River valley even though he seemed unusually reticent about discussing his former life. Occasionally he alluded to travels in Ireland, Scotland and the West Indies. He avoided strangers, and except for a kind of furtiveness, his conduct seemed exemplary.

In time, Dr. Wilson left the little school to begin a medical practice in nearby Newfane, and the residents of Brookline and its outlying communities of Grassy Brook, Lily Pond and Hedgehog Hill sought another teacher. Dr. Wilson developed an excellent reputation as a physician. But all was not well. A Boston newspaper printed the confession of one Michael Martin, alias Captain Lightfoot, who was hanged in that year for a crime in Boston. The confession was long and lugubrious and dealt in detail with the infamous careers of himself and his partner, a notorious Captain Thunderbolt. Michael Martin told of their adventures as highwaymen in Scotland and Ireland and how, with Captain Thunderbolt shot in the leg, they had barely managed to escape with their lives to the West Indies.

1836 octagonal schoolhouse near Little Creek, Delaware

Tongues wagged and soon Dr. Wilson found the valley no longer to his liking. In 1836 he moved to Brattleboro and built a home so secluded that it could be called a hideout. At his death it was revealed that he had a huge scar on the calf of his leg, and by his bed were three English double-barreled guns, three pairs of brass-bound pistols, several swords and most damning of all — ten heavy gold watches.

The architecture? Classical in nature because of its no-nonsense utilitarian form.

A CARRIAGE HOUSE

*New York City
carriage house detail*

*Row of handsome New York
City carriage houses*

For most Americans, the barn served as a carriage house. But urban and suburban Americans built special houses to shelter their precious animals and carriages. Wealthier citizens built carriage houses that included quarters for grooms and even grooms' families. Grooms were servants who drove the carriages, fed and curried the horses and kept the phaetons, landaulets, sulkies, sleds and a whole lexicography of other equipment in gleaming condition. If the groom was employed by a very wealthy family, he wore distinctive livery, or uniform, to match footmen, butlers and others of the household staff. Emily Post's original book on etiquette gives valuable advice to those about to adapt the family colors to the uniforms of liveried servants while Thorstein Veblen's treatise, *The Theory of the Leisure Class,* lumped all that under "conspicuous consumption" and vulgar display.

A carriage house was arranged so that the top floor held hay and grain, hoisted through the opening beneath the pulley arm. Chutes inside the carriage house conveyed the hay and grain as needed to the stables below. Stables were located at the rear of the building at the lowest ground level, and the main floor at the front level held the carriages. The groom's quarters were off to one side of the main floor and were usually heated by a stove.

Carriage houses smelled of timothy, horses, neat's-foot oil, saddle soap, leather, oats, salt hay, unpainted wood, enameled and lacquered carriages, kerosene and tallow. That fragrant combination was matched by the sounds of sleigh bells, creaking leather, squeaking hickory, stomping hoofs, itinerant blacksmiths' tools and irate Irish coachmen.

Today the carriage house has not outlived its usefulness and survives in number. Young couples, just married, are lucky to have a converted carriage house as their first home. It is home and garage and as it is often located off the main thoroughfare behind a large, old house, the carriage house is a pleasant place in which to live. Because the carriage houses were often substantially and fashionably built, they find favor as chemists' labs, artists' studios and antique shops.

City dwellers know that the old, row carriage houses make first-rate apartments and they now rent at prices that would be inconceivable to the original stable hands.

The tall, decorated carriage house to the right is located in Chatham, New Jersey, and is a fine example of a Gothic Revival building. Its pointed eaves and star-and-trefoil bargeboarding give it Gothic personality. The cupola, set askew at the juncture of the ridgelines, is a romantic era symbol of individuality and picturesqueness.

Phaeton

Landaulet

Governess cart

A MANSARD DEPOT

There was once a time when America's railroads displayed pride in their role in American life.

Whether it was brass or newly varnished walnut and maple, railroad equipment gleamed proudly across the states. The Lackawanna Railroad maintained three greenhouses to supply cut flowers for its dining cars. Acres of land were put aside to grow shrubs and evergreens to spruce up the approaches to the railroad stations, terminals and junctions.

America's finest architects were retained to build railroad stations and a colorful array of building then became part of our heritage. Depots in the Gothic, Mansard, Italianate, Romanesque, Shingled, Renaissance, Tudor and other styles made rich contribution to the personalities of America's cities and towns.

The railroads tried to make their stations suitable to the communities they serviced. University towns often have stations of the Collegiate Gothic style. Other stations reflect the fashions of the years in which they were built. We can tell from the Mansard style of architecture that the station in the painting was built in the 1880s.

The passenger station was managed by a passenger agent who lived with his family on the third floor. The second floor was given over to business and the first floor was devoted to ticket offices and the comfort of travelers. The station agent had a busy time of it. He was telegrapher, manager and business agent. In his third floor bedroom was another telegraphic key which kept him in touch with railroad traffic twenty-four hours a day. Most agents and their families could sleep through the clacking of the keys, but became instantly alert at code initials preceding a message meant for them.

Today, because of curtailed service, many of the apartments, which were formerly the homes of the depot masters, are rented to people who find them convenient places to live. Other depots have become civic centers, libraries and useful boons to our communities.

Railroad stations fall into four categories. The largest, situated at the terminus of the system, are called "terminals." At the crossing of railroad lines, the stations are called "junctions" and the tiniest stations are designated as "shelters." The stations located along the lines are designated as "stations," even though nearby residents refer to them as "depots."

Our lonely looking station is in Hopewell, New Jersey, not far from the great university at Princeton. The Reading Railroad built the large Mansard passenger station in brick in anticipation of a lively growth of the town. Hopewell's assets are in beauty and history. "Progress" never quite happened.

Catskill Mountains station in the American shingle style

A FLOUNDER HOUSE

Alexandria, Virginia, is, in its older sections, almost a museum of early American architectural types. Houses of the Federal and Greek Revival styles are kept in fine condition by their owners, many of whom are involved in matters of State in Washington, D.C., just across the Potomac. In a ramble through the cobblestone streets that slope down to the harbor, we find a number of houses, basically Federal in design, which seem to have been involved in some kind of accident.

The flounder house, or half-house as it is known outside of Alexandria, is not an accident, but a deliberate design based on a need that still remains a mystery. The houses were obviously intended some day to be finished in symmetrical form, but because other houses were built directly next door, they can never be completed. The "unfinished" or blank side of the house is usually on the property line, although some houses have the blank side facing the rear.

The reason suggested for the shape of the flounder house is that when the land for the town was auctioned off in 1749, every purchaser had to build on his property within a specified two-year period or the land reverted back to the town. The half-house was constructed as the rear wing of a larger house to be built later as family and fortune increased. The half-house was, if this theory is correct, a hurried measure to secure the deed. But our knowledge of architecture tells us that the prevailing architectural style of the flounder house is the Federal style of the first quarter of the nineteenth century. This makes the story of the land auctions of 1749 somewhat unlikely.

Another explanation offered is that sometime in the early nineteenth century, Alexandria had some form of restrictive ordinance with zoning and subdivision controls which impetuous builders thought might be repealed. The builders built, the laws held firm, and the property on which the other half of the flounder house was to go went to another builder who built and thus made permanent the odd shape of the house of his neighbor.

Other theories? Some say that the flounder house was a local builder's variation of a row house to be added to as tenants developed. And then there's always the story of the window tax to fall back on.

Whatever the answer to the origins of the flounder house, it gives Alexandria's Federal formality a charming counterpoint.

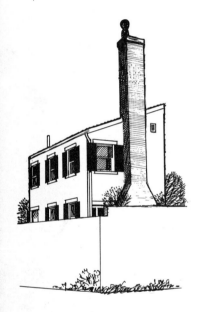

Walled flounder house

A GATEHOUSE

A gatehouse was originally a shelter for a guard who challenged anyone seeking admission to a walled or fenced domain. Guards, armed with pikes and halberds, were attended by fierce mastiffs, huge bone-crushing dogs. If a guard attends a gatehouse today, he is usually armed with a telephone to announce the arrival of visitors.

Late nineteenth and early twentieth century architects delighted in the creation of gatehouses for their wealthiest clients. With the hard work of designing the mansion behind him, the architect could expend a little pent-up whimsy on the gatehouse. For this reason gatehouses tend to be colorful while still reflecting the personality of the house within the gates.

The fairy-tale house shown here was built in 1930 to attract people to a new community of fine houses. The community was called "Wychwood" and the houses tried hard to live up to the name.

Bernhardt Müller was commissioned to build the fanciful house, and with some help from medieval models he gave Wychwood an atmosphere worthy of the Black Forest — the brothers Grimm would have been delighted. The house reaches back five centuries to the houses of the walled cities which compressed their buildings into the tall, picturesque shapes suggested by our gatehouse here.

Wychwood carried its fairy-tale theme to street posts, letter boxes and weather vanes, and the design of these objects was turned over to a man thoroughly qualified in that special area.

In 1929 John Bennett wrote *The Pigtail of Ah Lee Ben Loo*,* a collection of children's stories written over a forty-year period. Mr. Bennett illustrated his book with silhouettes inspired by the German artist, Paul Konewka, who was influenced by the flavor of medieval German towns still decorating the German countryside.

These illustrations in turn provided the inspiration for the iron silhouettes that decorate turrets, fence posts and any other objects too obviously twentieth century. The book has long been out of print, but its pictures live on in Wychwood.

The community, which began its life in the difficult days of the depression, has weathered bad times and changing tastes to become a model of successful planning. There is still a touch of romance in all of us.

*Longmans, Green and Co.

A TOWN HOUSE

The little house at No. 75½ Bedford Street is drenched in literary, dramatic and musical history. For here, in the narrowest house in New York City, have lived some of the most celebrated names in the arts.

As a young tenant, Lionel Barrymore achieved his first success on stage at the Cherry Lane Theatre once just around the corner. It was here that Deems Taylor composed the music for Edna St. Vincent Millay's *The King's Henchman* which was performed at the Metropolitan Opera House uptown a way.

But No. 75½ is best known as the early home of Edna St. Vincent Millay. For a generation of readers in the 1920s and '30s, Miss Millay represented freedom and daring and the kind of mystique that Greenwich Village still holds for many. She was also one of America's great poets.

The little town house is only 9′6″ wide as it was built in the driveway of the older house next door. Visitors must use the back door of the house as the front door enters directly into a kitchen. The stepped gables give the building an old Nieu Amsterdam look, and the original brick is almost obscured by layer after layer of paint. The painting is of the back of No. 75½ because the Bedford Street facade is almost indistinguishable from its neighbors.

The architecture? Neo Nieu Amsterdam.

A CONTINUING BARN

Throughout the New England states a good number of houses and their connecting barns still stretch over the rocky countryside. Age and fire are steadily reducing their number and New Englanders are forbidden by law to build replacements. Along with icehouses, carriage houses, railroad shanties, gatehouses and camp-meeting houses, they are part of the vanishing American scene.

The fires and the laws are related. The long succession of barns and houses acts as a flue so that barn fires beginning at one end will soon consume the other.

New England farmers discovered early that the severe snowstorms of the region made tending cattle, sheep, horses and pigs a difficult task. By attaching barns to each other as need grew, the farmer could care for his livestock and be handy to his grain without ever having to brave the snows. The convenience apparently overcame other disadvantages. Odors drifting to the family eating in the kitchen reminded them of the pigs at one end of the barns, and when bacon was frying, the pigs at the other end might be equally distressed.

Our continuing barn on the next two pages is north of Bennington, Vermont. The yellow house was originally Greek Revival, but with the addition of a bay window with decorative cresting along the ridge, a later style was incorporated.

The little bay window with its spiky ornamentation is not a functional aspect of the building. Almost everything a farmer builds is of a highly functional order, but because he is human, the farmer somewhere, in cupolas, hex signs, and so forth, expresses his humanness in decoration.

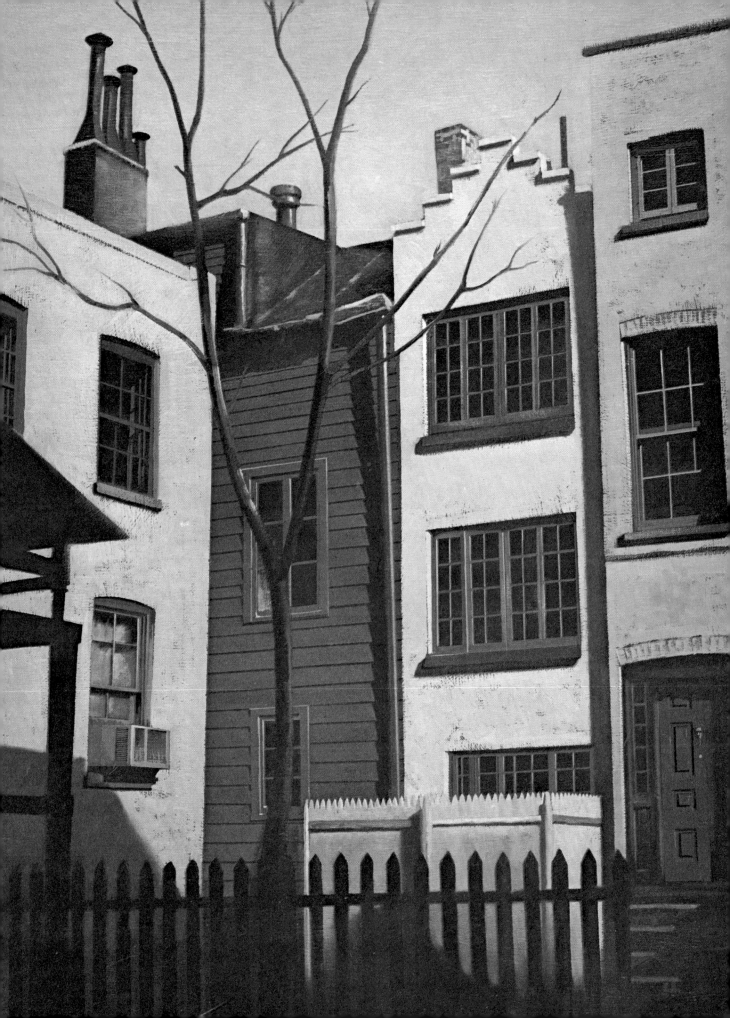

AN ICEHOUSE

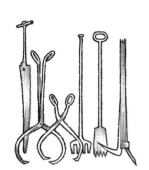

Icehouse tools: saws, tongs, chippers and an ice hook

Icehouse built into hillside

Washington Irving's chapel-style icehouse at Sunnyside

In 1827, a remarkably vital little Englishwoman named Frances Trollope arrived in America. In the next three years she traveled the nation, founded an unsuccessful department store in Cincinnati and wrote a book called *Domestic Manners of the Americans*. The book was published in England several years after Mrs. Trollope's return and was an instant sensation. Its publication restored the widow Trollope to financial independence, but it caused such a furor in America that it threatened to destroy Anglo-American relations.

Mrs. Trollope didn't have a lot to say about American manners that was commendable, but she did admire our ice. She noted with relish that every hotel and tavern had, in every season, huge quantities of ice to serve with food and drink. She was pleased to discover that the house she had rented outside of Cincinnati had an icehouse "that never failed."

Where ice was especially essential, in fishing villages and in hotels where food had to be stored, the icehouse had early become a standard structure.

Icehouses were built in many forms. Some were built into the sides of hills so that the earth itself became the insulator. Thomas Jefferson built his icehouse beneath a section of a covered walk that stretches out from his Monticello. It is circular and is covered with a deep cone of earth.

Most icehouses look like barns without windows. They were constructed with double walls and roofs, with about fourteen inches between the sheaths. Sawdust was poured between the walls and made effective insulation against outside heat.

In winter, ice was cut from lakes, ponds, and rivers by teams of men using saws, hooks and other specialized tools developed for the work. The men wore spiked soles strapped on their boots and horses were similarly equipped. Blocks of ice, typically 24″ thick by 48″ by 72″, were slid onto sleds and hauled away to the icehouses to be hoisted into the interior. The ice was placed in layers and separated by layers of sawdust. The whole was then covered with sawdust and was now ready for the hottest months ahead.

Our little icehouse was built to service a large home in Cape May, New Jersey. The electric refrigerator and the pollution of lakes have made it and its fellows obsolete, so that now we see them infrequently. A few generations ago, they were everywhere; their dark, cool interiors, packed with crystal clear ice and damp, fragrant sawdust, were a delight to the young ones. But that's progress.

We haven't been altogether fair to Mrs. Trollope. In time, Americans, understanding themselves a little better, treated the lady more kindly. Mark Twain championed her reporting and wrote that she had written fairly. "She neither gilded nor whitewashed us." Besides, Mrs. Trollope gave us some remarkable sons — one, Anthony, became a great nineteenth century novelist.

A CAMP-MEETING HOUSE

There was once a kind of camp meeting that was so primitive that Mrs. Trollope described it as bedlam.

The camp meeting that Mrs. Trollope reported was in a clearing deep in an Indiana forest in 1829. The preachers were of dubious character and the kind of religion imparted to the frontier people was of a highly unorthodox mold. "Sinners" rolled around in sawdust, sobbed, shrieked, moaned and otherwise shocked Mrs. Trollope's refined sensibilities.

An entirely different kind of camp meeting flourished in the middle of the nineteenth century. It served not only as a place of religious refurbishment, but also, to many families, as an escape from city life. Families too poor to afford regular summer vacations could afford the camp meeting. Whole church congregations, in wagons loaded with tents and camping equipment, would travel in a haze of dust from the heat of the city to some quiet wooded area served by a spring or clear stream.

Tents were erected and once or twice a day religious meetings were held. The rest of the time was spent in cooking, singing and, if the denomination approved, playing baseball.

As the years went by, some of these camps became permanent establishments. Central meeting houses, doubling as mess halls, were erected and a few small buildings to house the clergy were situated on the perimeter of the camp.

Camp-meeting house neighbor

In Chautauqua County, New York, a very famous camp meeting developed. It was originally a camp for the study of the Bible, but it eventually evolved into an institution to cover the whole field of education.

The outdoor lectures at Chautauqua, which came to be called "Chautauquas," attracted distinguished lecturers from all over the world and served handsomely to spread enlightenment in a young nation hungry for learning.

The gingerbread camp-meeting house in the painting is a fine example of its kind in its final stage of development. Eventually, tents were replaced with these picturesque little houses that would shelter a family over the summer. This wonderfully decorated cottage is over a hundred years old and is below the Mason-Dixon Line in South Seaville, New Jersey. The ground that the cottage stands on belongs to the Methodist Church, but the cottage belongs to a Methodist minister. There are no windows on one side of the cottage, but four on the other. The camp is arranged as a quadrangle with many equally charming cottages forming the outer perimeter. In the center is the meeting hall with a prominent bell to call the campers to worship.

In 1969, South Seaville saw its 106th annual camp meeting and, if the condition of the little cottage is an indication, there will be many more. Ministers on summer vacation come from southern New Jersey, roll up their sleeves, and for a while become carpenters, masons and painters. The results are spiritually and esthetically rewarding.

A SHANTY

The crossing watchman's shanty is now a rarity. Overhead roads, electronic devices and automatic gates have displaced the watchman who once stopped traffic at the approach of a train.

Railroading has a romantic appeal, and almost every phase of it can create a nostalgia for those old enough to remember when the railroad was king.

The shanty is the most humble house in this book, but an older generation can accurately recall this kind of shack with its little iron stove and attached coal shed. The captain's chair leaning against the shanty is as important to the correctness of the nostalgic dream as the cross-buck crossing sign. And almost always there was a lumberyard nearby.

Before the invention of automatic couplings, freight and passenger trains had to be joined or separated by hand. Accidents were inevitable, and men crippled by these and other mishaps were given jobs as crossing watchmen. In a previous generation, many of the watchmen were wooden-legged Civil War veterans possessed of explosive vocabularies used unsparingly on any teamster who might be tempted to try his luck against the watchman's warning.

The crossing watchman's duty was to make the crossing safe for traffic and he used a variety of tools in his work. At busy intersections he cranked the striped and counterweighted crossing arms that blocked or opened the way for vehicles. At lesser crossings he was equipped with a staff on which was mounted a STOP sign. At night he swung a kerosene lantern.

On some of the railroad lines where traffic was infrequent, the crossing watchman put his lonely hours to use by planting and tending a vegetable or flower garden on the railroad property. Huge tomatoes and magnificent flowers were often the result. Great care and the gleanings of the cattle cars had much to do with his success.

The shanty is so simple that we can hardly consider it worthy of architectural discussion. The wooden siding has undergone much replacement since the original board-and-batten construction shown over the doorway.

A PATTERN-ENDED HOUSE

Englishmen emigrating to America in the mid-eighteenth century felt homesick for their native land. They named towns after their places of birth and, whenever they could, they built in a way to remind themselves of home. Englishmen coming from the Surrey-Essex district of England built a very special reminder.

In the fifteenth century, artisans from Flanders and France had introduced into the Surrey-Essex area a flamboyant kind of brickwork which, when applied to the gable end of a house, made that house a pattern-ended house. Glazed blue-white bricks were set in among the salmon pink bricks to form ellipses, triangles, flowers and diaper designs.

The tradition came over the seas with Surrey-Essex settlers and wherever they settled in the new nation, their handsome, ornate patterns flourished. Most of the pattern-enders that have survived are near the Delaware Bay area, although there are still a few survivors as far south as New Orleans.

By far, the largest numbers were built in the southwest corner of New Jersey, a state remarkably indifferent to its architectural inheritance. The splendid pattern-ended house shown here has survived neglect and the plundering of its once beautiful interior paneling only because a distinguished architect couldn't bear to watch its disintegration. Painstakingly he has worked to bring the house back to its former beauty. That it is the most exuberant of all the pattern-ended houses is beyond question, but its enormous value in terms of heritage has eluded official circles.

The Dickinson house was built in 1754 in Salem County, New Jersey, not far from a busy colonial glassworks at Wistarburgh, for John and Martha Dickinson. A variant of the name John is Ian and that's why the initials read "I and M D". The house originally had a gambrel roof, but the upper floors were enlarged to accommodate boarders in a brief boat building boom during the Civil War. Old photographs show that the flat roof and brackets of that remodeling made it look Italianate. In 1931 an attempt to restore it changed the flat roof into a peaked one which gave it a more authentic, but not the original, look.

The Dickinson house is difficult to find. It is far off any main roads and the countryside is wild and a bit desolate—all of which may have contributed to a tragic part of the house's history. The fifteen-year-old daughter of a former owner of this house was murdered in such a grisly manner that when the funeral of the victim was held, more than a thousand people gathered on the lawn of the home. The pattern-ended gaiety must have seemed sadly out of place.

The decorated end of the house faces west. On certain evenings, the setting sun can give the lovely coral brick and the antique designs such a glowing beauty that New Jersey should be proud to claim it.

AN OCTAGON HOUSE

We can never think of an octagon house without thinking of Orson Squire Fowler, the New York farm boy who reversed a trend at the height of the American romantic era (1820-1900).

Orson Squire Fowler was a student at Amherst College in Massachusetts when he and his classmate, Henry Ward Beecher, journeyed to Boston to hear a lecture by an Italian phrenologist. Phrenology is a pseudo-science which pretends to read the character of an individual by the shape of the head. Phrenology also attempts to predict the future. Romantic era people loved that sort of thing. The lecture made a tremendous impression on Orson Squire Fowler and in time he became the leading phrenologist in the country. Henry Ward Beecher was unimpressed and went his way to become, in his time, America's most famous preacher.

Mr. Fowler became wealthy as a phrenological lecturer and reader and even wealthier as the author of *Phrenology Proved, Illustrated and Applied* which saw sixty-two editions. Mr. Fowler sold a lot of books.

Our hero, not content to be an authority on the shape of the head, decided that America needed a new look architecturally. As the head of his own publishing firm, he wrote a book on a revolutionary kind of place to live in, the octagon house. He called his book *A Home for All, or The Gravel Wall and Octagon Mode of Building*. His book was a great success.

The octagon house was to be a simple and direct building, utilizing all the benefits that mathematics, nature and physics gave the octagon. Orson Squire Fowler was proposing "organic" or "form-follows-function" building, a precept of modern architecture. His readers were so caught up in his idea that between 1850 and 1853 there was a building boom of octagonal, dodecagonal and round houses.

The mathematical logic and the restraint of the simple octagon house make it a classical expression in a romantic era — a reversal of a trend by a man who knew no classical restraint when he built his own octagon. The Fowler house in Fishkill, New York, contained a hundred rooms, two gymnasiums and was five stories high with a 20′ x 20′ glass-roofed cupola!

This house, sometimes called "The Bonnet House," belongs to the distinguished author, Carl Carmer, who writes wonderful books on rivers and places and, with Mrs. Carmer, books for children. The house was built at Irvington-on-Hudson by a wealthy tea merchant, and the interior of the house reflects the merchant's oriental connections.

The house has an octagonal gazebo and a lovely ghost. But that's Carl Carmer's story. In his book, *My Kind of Country,** Mr. Carmer has written lovingly of the ghost who haunts his house and of Orson Squire Fowler, the inventor of America's first original form of architecture.

*David McKay Company, Inc. (c) 1966 Carl Carmer

Classic octagon with Doric pillars and pilasters, Laceyville, Pennsylvania

In Wilmington, Vermont, a board-and-batten octagon house has sprouted wings.

OLANA, A ROMANTIC HOUSE

If the romantic era needed a monument, Olana could serve the purpose admirably. The building and its builder are exquisite examples of American romanticism. Olana is Oriental and from its "place on high" views breathtaking miles of river and mountains. Its builder was an adventuring Hudson River school painter whose talents, daring, good looks and success made him an idol of the waning era.

Frederick Edwin Church traveled the world in search of the incredible landscapes he produced so profitably. In the time of the Hudson River school painters, the public paid admission to gaze in astonishment at the huge landscapes and marvel at the scenes made so commonplace today by photography. Police had to handle the crowds that collected to see his *Heart of the Andes* painting. Admission fees sometimes totaled $3,000 in a month. Church was acclaimed by art critics all over the world and a romantically oriented public took his paintings to its heart.

In 1868, Mr. Church and his family traveled to the Holy Land and in the best tradition of nineteenth century adventurers, hired a Syrian dragoman, a cook and a photographer. Then, with his family safely housed, Mr. Church embarked on a journey by camel caravan to the mysterious, lost, rose-red city of Petra. Meals were served in darkened, deserted desert towers on beautiful white tablecloths with cut glass and shining silver. To make matters dangerous was the fact that the Bedouin inhabitants of the land around Petra looked with anger on any graven images — and Frederick Church had come to paint! Already one European artist had been murdered while drawing the luminous Greco-Roman buildings carved out of the living stone.

A robber-chief and an Arab headman, loaded down with weapons, accompanied the party. At the site of Petra, which can only be approached through a narrow cleft in the rocks, Church sketched the fantastic scene surrounded by additional bodyguards armed with flintlocks and clubs.

The painting that Mr. Church produced from his sketches now hangs in Olana, the dream house he built from the memories of his travels. Seen from the bridge that spans the Hudson, Olana seems more a dream than a house. And Olana is more than a house — it's a reflection of a romantic era of American culture.

Olana, which means "our place on high," stands above a beautiful slope to the Hudson River at Hudson, New York, on the very spot where Henry Hudson gave up his search for a path to the Indies.

Olana seemed doomed just a few years ago. The story of the triumph of a handful of people who cared enough to preserve Olana for the generations of the future is too lengthy to be given proper honor in these pages. It is comforting to know that New York State's Taconic State Park Commission will care for it in perpetuity. It is open to the public and it is a rewarding place to visit.

A HOUSE OF WORSHIP

When Minard Lafever was eighteen years old, he built his first house. In his earlier teens, in real Horatio Alger fashion, he had walked almost fifty miles from his home near Watkins Glen to Geneva, New York to buy his first book on architecture. Until 1830, when he was thirty-two years old, one of America's most influential architects was content to call himself a carpenter. As America had no schools of architecture, it was left largely to the individual to adopt whatever title modesty and common sense would allow.

When Minard Lafever's first book, *The Young Builder's General Instructor,* was published in 1829, he at last decided that he had earned the right to call himself an architect and directly launched himself into America's building boom of the 1830s with great distinction. His early constructions were almost all in the fashionable Greek Revival style, but in time his greatest works were to be outstanding examples of Gothic church architecture.

In 1938 one of the worst hurricanes to strike the northeastern U.S. created havoc from Maine to Virginia. One of the areas hit hardest was Sag Harbor, Long Island, where incredible damage occurred. Next to the loss of life, the saddest word to come out of Sag Harbor was the news that the well-loved Whalers' Church had lost the towering steeple that had served as a mariners' landmark since it was built with reverence by ships' carpenters in 1843.

Even without its spyglass steeple, the Whalers' Presbyterian Church is a fascinating building. Lafever built other houses in the immediate area in the Greek manner, but for the daring whaling men who commissioned the church, he chose a style which had been introduced into Europe and later America as a result of Napoleon's expedition to the Nile. Although the Emperor's adventure was a military fiasco, it was culturally profitable. Napoleon's officers found the Rosetta Stone, unlocking the secrets of ancient hieroglyphics. More important to this story, these same officers made drawings of tombs and temples which fired the imagination of romantic era Europeans and Americans.

Before the hurricane of 1938

Suddenly, Egyptian-inspired architecture seemed wonderfully suitable for "profound" construction. The Egyptian style was used for cemetery gateways and was considered solemnly ideal for prisons. The romantic era was full of surprises!

Lafever designed the decorations along the crest of the building to resemble whalers' flencing spades which are blades on long handles used to cut blubber from the animals. Inside the church, moldings were designed to look like rope, and whalers' spears are used decoratively. The outside of the church is covered in white-painted cedar shingles which give the building a beautifully textured surface. The mood, the labor, the materials, and Mr. Lafever's fee all cost $17,000.

A GAZEBO

Near Paris, an exquisite Oriental folie—French for gazebo

The dictionary instructs us to pronounce gazebo GUH-*ZEE*-BO. If we say GUH-*ZAY-BO*, we are alluding to that undesirable character, the wise guy. Some dictionaries also point out that the word had its origin in a gazing room and that would explain why gazebos are almost always placed to face a pleasant view.

The octagonal gazebo shown here is meant to represent a Mississippi riverboat pilot house. It was built by the sister-in-law of Mark Twain as a retreat for the author and he loved it. It was originally open to the elements, but was later glassed in and the fireplace added.

Mark Twain wrote *Huckleberry Finn* and *Tom Sawyer* in this gazebo and later he wrote nostalgically of the flashing storms he could watch gathering in the Chemung Valley, in upper New York State.

The architectural detailing is roughly suggestive of the Gothic. The cross-buck patterning of wood on its sides is a favorite Victorian device and is used in other architectural forms of the period.

Our gazebo now stands on the campus of Elmira College, the oldest degree-conferring women's college in America.

Exotic octagon gazebo at octagon house

A LIGHTHOUSE

Late Victorian era lighthouse, privately owned and operated, to guide family's racing sloops. Biloxi, Miss.

George Washington started America's first lighthouse service and it grew until the nation could once boast of 527 lighthouses ranging its coastlines and great lakes. Only 180 lighthouses still are manned by crews, and automation is steadily whittling down that number.

Lighthouses are usually run by a uniformed keeper and two Coast Guard seamen. The light itself is operated by electric motors powered by diesel generators. The 1,000-watt, 100,000 candlepower bulbs are magnified so intensely that the focused beams may be seen twenty miles away. The prisms and mirrors, clean and polished, are beautiful objects made of cut glass mounted in brass. Prisms must be covered with cloth in the daylight hours as the sun's rays, focused through the magnifying lenses, would cause disastrous fires.

Each lighthouse has its own distinctive flash and hornblast to identify itself to passing ships. The oldest lighthouse in America, on Little Brewster Island in Boston Harbor, has a seven-second flash every half minute.

The reader will have arrived at our Block Island, Rhode Island, lighthouse when, on a foggy day, he hears a five-second blast every thirty seconds. On a clear night, our octagonal lighthouse will flash a green light for thirty-seven hundredths of a second every 3.7 seconds. It is called the South East Light and it sits high on Monhegan Bluff, reflecting the architectural era in which it was built — the 1870s.

AN OUTHOUSE

Many kinds of structures at one time known to everyone have all but disappeared from the American scene. The once familiar icehouse is now so rare that to find one might take a whole day of travel. What mechanical refrigeration did to icehouses, modern plumbing has done to the outhouse. The outhouse was once an appendage to every home. Every part of the country had its own name for it. It was called a "necessary," a "privy," the "outback," a "Chick Sales." The last was in honor of a comedian by that name who made a career of humor surrounding the outhouse. The outhouse was usually a very simple structure set at such a length from the main house as to be a compromise of convenience and sanitation.

Sometimes the little houses were made to relate architecturally to the houses that they were parted from. Not far from the Model Home pictured on page 7, there stood a Gothic mansion with a beautiful outhouse, frothy with carpenter's lace. The interior was wood and plaster with all the cusps, finials and pendants that the Gothic Revival imagination could supply.

Mr. Jefferson's privy at Monticello is also set into a wall.

In New Market, New Jersey, Duncan Phyfe of furniture fame built his daughter a Greek Revival house as a wedding present, and the little classical outhouse that went with it still survives.

One of the first people in the nation to advocate indoor plumbing was our old friend, Orson Squire Fowler, who incorporated the running water system into his 100-room octagon house in Fishkill. His neighbors thought him odd, but he was just a little ahead of his time.

The outhouse we show here was chosen because it was designed by Thomas Jefferson and is part of the famous serpentine walls of the University of Virginia.

There are a number of these privies on the grounds. All are set into the curving walls and all are identical. They have, of course, been replaced by modern facilities, but they still serve as handy repositories for lawn mowers and the tools to service them.

The style of these little houses is classical as is the design of all the handsome buildings on the University grounds. The privies also act as anchors for the serpentine walls which, on one side, provide paths to college buildings, and on the other, enclose lovely gardens. The walls themselves are only the thickness of one brick and the purpose of the curves is not for picturesqueness, which would be romantic, but for rigidity.

Duncan Phyfe built this "necessary" for his daughter in 1814. The house that went with it is Greek Revival.

It is strange to reflect that one who builds in the classical revival mode, as Mr. Jefferson did, is actually a romanticist. For it is a fact that those who strive to revive a bygone era are romanticists. Just to the left of the opening of the colonnade, in the background of the picture, was the room of Edgar Allan Poe, the arch-romantic of the literary world.

A FIRE-ENGINE HOUSE

Anthemion from Parthenon

In his beautifully researched book about architecture in Brooklyn Heights, New York,* Clay Lancaster refers to a "handsome little fire-engine house with Renaissance details built in 1903." The description proved to be delightfully accurate, and Clay Lancaster's elegant firehouse has been chosen to represent its kind for a number of reasons.

Brooklyn Heights profited from the services of many of America's best nineteenth century architects and many of the names appearing in the pages of this book have had a rendezvous with history here. Orson Squire Fowler's friend, preacher Henry Ward Beecher, preached in the Italianate style Plymouth Church. Minard Lafever, who designed the Egyptianate Whalers' Church, designed many of the Heights homes in the Greek Revival style and the Church of the Holy Trinity in the Gothic style. The redoubtable Mrs. Trollope made note of the Brooklyn Collegiate Institute for Young Ladies.

The style of architecture called Renaissance Revival has not been previously mentioned. Our fire-engine house is an excellent example of this style with its abundant classical ornamentation. Since the building has a slanting Mansard roof, the style can be pinpointed as French Renaissance. The details of each floor are different from its neighbor, although all the details are derived from Roman and Greek classical elements. Heavy balustrades, instead of iron railings, and windows with half-round arches give it even more of a Renaissance pedigree. The decorations at the extremities of the eaves are called "anthemions."

The paired buildings to the left of our fire-engine house are former carriage houses converted into a home and a sculptor's studio.

Fire-engine house in Goshen, New York, reflects character of the town. Lookout tower is also used for drying out hoses.

The ceiling of the ground floor of the fire-engine house still has hooks where once automatic harness was dropped onto waiting horses below at the sound of the alarm. The stalls that once held horses have been cemented over and two brilliant red fire engines now stand in tandem.

Most buildings are, for better or worse, cultural expressions. By understanding the meaning behind the symbols of architecture, we can vastly increase our understanding of ourselves and our history. There is considerable evidence that we are entering a new romantic era. Once again young men are wearing long hair while their elders are gingerly toying with beards, sideburns and moustaches; symphony orchestras are being conducted in bravura style; concert pianists have abandoned mathematically precise keyboard techniques for passionate interpretations; the classical, international mode of architecture is grudgingly yielding to warmer and more humanistic creations; a new interest has grown in the pseudo-sciences such as astrology, mind reading, etc., and the young are enthralled by their own kind of sentimental ballad. A backward glance at the old romantic era will give us some insight to what lies ahead.

*Old Brooklyn Heights: New York's First Suburb, Charles E. Tuttle Co.

THE CLASSIC AND THE ROMANTIC

What Kind of a House Is That? often refers to the "classic" and "romantic" styles of architecture. To understand these styles, they must be viewed in relation to the mood of the times in which they flourished. The classic Greek Revival structures that Americans built in the 1830s, while classic in form, were actually romantic expressions. This seeming contradiction is resolved when the reader understands that one of the qualities of a romanticist is a yearning to recreate the past. In many ways buildings are a monument to a mood. A fine definition of the qualities of the classic and the romantic is found in *The Humanities* by Louise Dudley and Austin Faricy.*

"The qualities that characterize classicism are clarity, simplicity, restraint, objectivity and balance. The qualities that characterize romanticism are love of the remote and indefinite, escape from reality, lack of restraint in form and emotions, preference for picturesqueness or grandeur or passion. Classicism and romanticism are fundamentally in opposition; what is classic is not romantic, and what is romantic is not classic. The classic is restrained; the romantic is not restrained. The classic is finished, perfect; it has great beauty of form; the romantic is unfinished, imperfect, and often careless of form. The classic is simple, the romantic complex; the classic is objective, the romantic is subjective; the classic is finite, concerned only with projects that can be realized and accomplished; the romantic is infinite, concerned with plans that can never be realized, affecting 'thoughts coequal with the clouds.' "

*McGraw-Hill Book Co.